SONIA ALLISON'S
BREAD BOOK

SONIA ALLISON'S
BREAD BOOK

PIATKUS

© 1983 Sonia Allison

First published in 1983 by Judy Piatkus (Publishers) Limited
of Loughton, Essex

British Library Cataloguing in Publication Data

Allison, Sonia
    Sonia Allison's bread book
    1. Bread
    I. Title
    641.8'15   TX769

ISBN 0-86188-166-4

Designed by Paul Sanders
Cover designed by Ken Leeder

Typeset by Gilbert Composing Services, Leighton Buzzard
Printed and bound by The Pitman Press, Bath

CONTENTS

INTRODUCTION

If one glances through works by past writers and poets, bread and love appear synonymous. Jonathan Swift concluded, 'Bachelor's fare; bread and cheese, and kisses'. Thackeray relates the tale of Werther in *Sorrows of Werther:*

> 'Werther had a love for Charlotte
> Such as words could never utter;
> Would you know how first he met her?
> She was cutting bread and butter.'

To take Swift and Thackeray seriously leads us to this conclusion: what better way of winning friends than by offering them the delights of homemade bread – with or without butter – with its warm and mellow crust, hearty flavour and distinctive texture?

Sliced and wrapped, convenient though it is for toast and sandwiches, is not the total answer where bread lovers and connoisseurs are concerned and it is for them that this little book has been written.

My choice is wide and varied and offers all the basic breads from white to brown; all the shapes one can think of, including a chimney pot loaf made in a clay flower pot; a wide selection of rolls; Irish Soda breads and others without yeast; a foreign assortment from Jewish Bagels and French sticks to Indian Chapati and Naan bread; puffed-up cakes; Danish pastries and Pizzas; classy Brioches and Croissants; fragrant fruit loaves; all manner of popular buns; even German Stollen which has proved so popular at Christmas along with a garland cake from Scandinavia, prettily white iced and decorated with cherries and seasonal novelties.

To set you on your way, I shall begin with hints and tips on choice of ingredients, continue with freezer facts and lead you into the recipes. At the end, I shall give you a list of the most common mistakes, backed up with reasons. Thus if you are confronted with a disappointment, you will understand why and not lose confidence and the incentive to try again. And if you do have problems slicing the bread, I leave you to dwell on this old proverb from Czechoslovakia: 'He who cannot cut the bread evenly, cannot get on well with people.'

Choosing Ingredients

Flour

Avoid self-raising flour which is basically wrong for two reasons:

1. The raising agent it contains will conflict with the yeast. (This does not apply to non-yeasted breads.)

2. The flour is on the soft side, probably milled from European wheat and therefore more suited to cake-making and biscuits.

Ideally, flour for yeast cookery should be plain white and marked *strong* as this is well endowed with a protein substance called gluten which has excellent powers of 'stretchability'. This, in turn, enables the loaf or rolls to rise to their maximum capacity without collapsing, and also produces a light and spongy texture. Strong flours are milled from hard wheats grown in North America and the USSR.

As alternatives to white, you can use brown flour which has had a minimal amount of bran and wheatgerm removed or, for really nutty-tasting and extra healthy bread, wholemeal or wholewheat flours which have had nothing added or taken away. One problem is that they produce heavier results than plain or brown flours but some people prefer the more substantial quality of baked goods made with what can only be described as a 'complete' flour. The dense texture may be overcome if these flours are mixed with a proportion of white flour: say about one-third to one-half.

Although other cereal flours may be used for bread making – oats, barley and rye for instance – they contain little or no gluten and therefore must be mixed with half white or brown flour if the finished loaf, rolls or buns are to rise satisfactorily. No amount of yeast, itself a natural raising agent, will be able to make a dough rise if it is lacking in gluten.

All flour should be stored in a cool, dry and dark atmosphere in a jar with a well fitting stopper, and not kept for too long.

Yeast
This is the traditional raising agent used for bread making and there are two kinds available:

1. *Dried.* More easy to find than fresh, dried yeast (granular form) is sold in tins or sachets from supermarket chains, grocery stores, health-food shops and some chemists. Left in its sealed container, it will keep fresh up to one year. Once opened, the yeast should be transferred to a *small* airtight container with lid where it will remain active for a maximum of 4 months. Unless you plan on doing a lot of yeast cooking, the small sachets are a more practical buy than the larger tins.

Because dried yeast is concentrated, you need less than if you were using fresh. Thus if a recipe calls for 1 oz (25 g) fresh yeast, the equivalent in dried would be ½ oz (15 g) or 1 level tablespoon. Dried yeast has to be reconstituted before use and this is done by mixing it with a little sugar, some of the measured liquid and leaving it to stand in a warm place for between 15 to 20 minutes or until frothy.

2. *Fresh.* Fresh yeast looks like putty in appearance – it has the same beige colour – and should break cleanly and smartly. It should also feel cool to the touch and firm. If put into a small plastic container with an airtight lid or tied loosely in a small polythene bag, the yeast will remain active and in good condition in a refrigerator for up to 2 weeks.

Fresh yeast can also be frozen and this is best done in 1 oz (25 g) amounts. Wrap each piece in cling film and freeze up to 6 weeks. Either leave to thaw for 20 to 30 minutes before using, or add from frozen to the warm liquid and blend until smooth. Stale yeast begins to turn brownish and loses its efficiency as a raising agent.

Note: For amounts to use of either dried or fresh yeasts, see individual recipes. As a general guide, 1 oz (25 g) fresh or ½ oz (15 g) dried is sufficient for 3 lb (about 1.35 kg) plain white flour used for simple white bread; double the amount is needed for wholemeal or wholewheat breads.

Salt
This helps to improve the flavour of yeasted goods and also prevents the yeast – which is a living organism – from working too quickly and spoiling the texture of the loaf, cake, rolls or buns. However, too much holds the yeast back and stops it from working properly, while too little produces a tacky dough which is difficult to handle. A standard proportion is 1 or 2 level teaspoons per 1 lb (450 g) of flour.

Sugar

A small amount of sugar, literally 1 or 2 teaspoons blended with the dried yeast and some of the measured liquid, acts as a catalyst and helps to speed up the chemical reaction with the flour. Thus the dough gets off to a good start and rises smoothly and evenly. If preferred, 1 or 2 level teaspoons honey or golden syrup may be added instead of sugar if using white flour, and treacle or molasses if you are using brown flour. The choice is yours and again, use as much as the recipe tells you and do not be over-generous. An excessive amount of sweetener initially retards the growth of the yeast and sometimes kills it altogether.

Fat/Oil

Fat or oil is used to enrich a dough and make the texture more silky. It also discourages staling. Butter, margarine, white cooking fat, lard or pure vegetable fats may be used and are generally rubbed into the flour. Corn, peanut or sunflower oil may be substituted if preferred and added with the other liquids (but oil makes white dough very slightly grey-looking). It is helpful to know that 1 tablespoon of oil is equivalent to ½ oz (15 g) of fat.

Liquid

The usual proportion for a basic dough is ½ pt (275 ml) to 1 lb (450g) flour. Usually the liquid is water for a plain dough but half milk (which adds to the nutritional value of the dough) and half water may be used if preferred. So can all milk. The temperature of the liquid should be just above blood heat (100°F or 38°C) and this is easily achieved by mixing two-thirds cold liquid with one-third boiling. It may also be useful to know that doughs made with all milk have a softer, browner crust than those made with water.

Eggs

These are added to enriched doughs for flavour, colour and extra nutritional value. Also the finished loaf, buns or cake will keep moister for a longer time.

Basic Techniques

1. Prepare yeast liquid as described in individual recipes.

2. Sift dried ingredients into bowl. Rub in fat if used. Toss in other dry ingredients as specified in the recipe.

3. Add yeast liquid, rest of liquid and oil (if used instead of fat), and beaten egg or eggs.

4. Mix to a dough with fingertips or a fork.

5. Turn out on to a floured surface and knead until smooth, elastic and no longer sticky. Allow about 10 minutes for white dough and 5 for brown. If dough remains sticky, work in a little extra flour.

6. If using the dough hook attachment of an electric mixer, pour the yeast liquid into mixer bowl first and then add the other ingredients. Run machine at lowest speed for about 2 minutes to form a dough. Increase speed to half power and run machine a further 2 to 3 minutes. Turn dough out on to a floured surface and knead by hand until smooth, allowing about 5 to 7 minutes.

7. After the dough is kneaded, it is usually left to 'prove', the technical term for allowing the dough to rise to at least twice its original size. Shape the dough into a ball, put it into a lightly oiled bowl and cover with an inverted oiled plate. Leave the bowl in a sink half-filled with hand-hot water for about 1 to 1½ hours (the water should reach at least two-thirds up the side of the bowl), or in the airing cupboard at a temperature of around 90°F or 32°C.

8. A long, slow rise has little effect on the finished result (other than to improve it). Allow:

a) 1½ to 2 hours at kitchen temperature in a covered bowl (65°F to 70°F or 18°C to 21°C).

b) 4 hours in a cool place such as a larder or pantry.

c) Up to 12 hours in a refrigerator (usually overnight).

If proving in the refrigerator, *halve* the quantity of yeast used to prevent over-rising. Dough that has risen too much is hard to handle and has a strong, yeasty flavour. Leave the dough to warm up to room temperature before shaping.

9. After the dough has risen, it should be 'punched down' or 'knocked back' which means re-kneading the dough in order to bring it back to its original size and smoothness, and break down air bubbles created by the action of the yeast. If omitted, the texture of the baked dough is likely to be peppered with holes and somewhat uneven. It should take no longer than about 5 minutes' kneading on a floured surface. Some recipes do not require a second kneading.

10. The dough should now be shaped according to requirements, put into or on to tins, covered with greased or oiled polythene (such as opened out bags) or greaseproof paper, and left in a warm place (no slow rising this time) until it puffs up and doubles in size; about ¾ to 1 hour for a large loaf and half that time for rolls and buns. Doughs with dried fruit and/or fat with eggs take a little longer to rise than plain ones.

11. To prepare tins for baking, grease well to prevent dough from sticking. A bland and white unsalted vegetable fat or lard is best for this and it should be melted first. After greasing, a light dusting of flour on the inside of tins or over the trays also encourages the easy removal of baked goods. In general, good quality non-stick bakeware needs no attention.

12. Baking times will be given in each basic recipe, but as a general guide, the plainer the dough the hotter the oven. This means a temperature of 450°F (230°C), Gas 8 for a simple white loaf and either 375°F or 400°F (190°C or 200°C), Gas 5 or 6 for richer doughs. The object of a hottish oven is to kill off the yeast fairly rapidly, otherwise it will go on working and the dough will rise up too much and then collapse on itself.

13. To check if the loaf is cooked through to the centre, turn it out on to a wire rack and tap the base with your knuckles. If it sounds hollow, then it needs no further baking. If not, stand on a baking tray and return it to the oven for an extra 5 to 12 minutes.

14. For crusty sides, remove loaf or loaves about 5 minutes before they are ready, than put on to a baking tray. Continue to bake a further 5 to 10 minutes, depending on size. To ensure a really crusty finish, stand a small roasting tin of hot water in the bottom of the oven while the bread is baking, then remove it about 10 minutes before the end.

Freezer Facts

Both uncooked dough and baked loaves, etc., freeze satisfactorily and below are some guidelines.

1. Use dried yeast for the dough in preference to fresh and *double* the amount given in the recipe.

2. Divide the kneaded but *unrisen* dough into manageable amounts (1 lb or 450 g batches for instance) and put into heavy-duty polythene bags, first oiled inside or brushed with melted fat. Tie securely to exclude as much air as possible. Freeze plain, uncooked doughs up to 1 month and enriched doughs up to 3 months.

3. To freeze risen dough, knead lightly to break down air bubbles. Put into oiled or greased polythene bags, tie tightly and freeze up to 2 weeks only.

4. To thaw, untie bag or bags and leave dough overnight in the refrigerator or 5 to 6 hours at kitchen temperature. Allow to rise until double in size then re-knead quickly, shape as desired and leave to rise in the warm until dough is light and puffy, and again double in size. Bake as directed in the recipe.

5. If freezing already baked goods which are enriched with milk, eggs and fat, wrap securely and freeze up to 3 months.

7. If freezing crusty French sticks and equally crusty rolls, wrap well and leave no longer than 1 week as the crusts will start to flake off.

8. To thaw baked goods, leave in their wrapping for 3 to 6 hours at room temperature, depending on size. Alternatively, thaw in the oven by re-wrapping the loaf, etc., in foil and heating through for ¾ hour at 400°F (200°C), Gas 6. For rolls, leave wrapped and thaw 1½ hours at room temperature. If preferred, foil-wrap as bread and thaw in the oven by heating through for ¼ hour at 450°F (230°C), Gas 8.

WHITE BREADS

This section offers a selection of plain, basic white breads and mixed rolls covering some of the most popular varieties. These range from Farmhouse and Cottage loaves to Coburgs and what are generally referred to as Danish — oblong loaves with lengthwise slits. A recipe for Quick White Bread has also been included, together with old-fashioned Norfolk Dumplings plus delicious teatime Muffins and Lardy Cake. For those into high fibre, I have especially put in a recipe for Bran Bread, and you will also find recipes for a Pizza base, Onion 'Pretzels', Hamburger Buns and novelty breads.

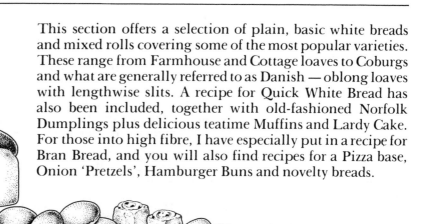

White Bread

Makes 3 large loaves

½ oz or 15 g (1 level tblsp) dried
  yeast with 2 level tsp caster
  sugar, honey or syrup OR
  1 oz (25 g) fresh yeast and
  no sugar
1½ pt (825 ml) warm water
  (mix ⅔ cold with ⅓
  boiling)
3 lb (1.35 kg) plain white
  strong flour
4-6 level tsp salt
1 level tblsp extra sugar
2 oz (50 g) fat or 4 tblsp salad
  oil

This recipe adapts easily into different shaped loaves.

1. Well-grease and flour 3 oblong loaf tins, each 2 lb or 900 g.

2. Mix dried yeast with sugar, honey or syrup and then add half the liquid. Leave in a warm place for about 15 minutes or until mixture foams up and looks like a glass of beer. Alternatively, blend water gradually into fresh yeast.

3. Sift flour and salt into a bowl. Toss in sugar. Rub in fat finely or otherwise make well in the centre of the dry ingredients and pour in the oil.

4. Add yeast liquid and remaining water *in one go* then mix to a dough with fork or fingertips. Draw together.

5. Turn out on to a floured surface and knead a good 10 minutes or until dough is smooth, elastic and no longer sticky. If necessary, work in a little extra flour.

6. Shape into a ball and put into a greased or oiled bowl. Cover with a greased or oiled plate and leave to rise until double in size. (See points 7 and 8 of Basic Techniques.)

7. Turn out on to a floured surface and knead briefly until smooth, elastic and no longer sticky. Divide equally into 3 pieces, shape to fit prepared tins and then dust lightly with flour. Cover with greased or oiled polythene or greaseproof paper and leave to rise in a warm place for ¾ to 1 hour or until light, puffy and at least double in size.

8. Bake for about ¾ hour just above oven centre set to 450°F (230°C), Gas 8. If tins are unable to sit on one shelf, bake two above oven centre and one below, changing them round at half time.

9. Leave in tins for 5 minutes then tap out on to wire cooling racks. Leave until cold.

10. For extra crunchy sides, remove loaves from oven 5 minutes early. Tap out on to a lightly greased and floured baking tray, turn the right way up and crispen in the oven for an extra 10 minutes. Cool completely on wire racks before storing in bread bins or freezing.

Farmhouse or Split Tin Loaves

Makes 3 large

Make exactly as previous recipe. After loaves have risen in tins, and just before baking, make a lengthwise cut in each and dust with flour. Bake exactly as white bread.

Coburg Loaves

Makes 3 large

Divide the risen dough into 3 equal pieces and shape into balls. Put on to 1 or 2 greased and floured baking trays. Dust with flour. Cover and leave to rise in the warm until double in size. With a sharp knife, make a cross cut on top of each. Dust with flour. Bake exactly as white bread.

Bloomer Loaves

Makes 3 large

Divide risen dough into 3 equal pieces and shape into 9-inch (22.5-cm) 'cigars' with pointed ends. Put on to 1 or 2 greased and floured baking trays then, with a sharp knife, make 6 diagonal slashes on top of each, about 1 inch (2.5 cm) apart. Brush with beaten egg. Cover and leave to rise in the warm until double in size. Bake exactly as white bread.

Cottage Loaves

Divide risen dough into 3 equal portions. Take one-third of dough off each. Shape the larger pieces into balls and stand on 1 or 2 greased and floured baking trays. Top with smaller pieces, also shaped into balls. Push a floured handle of a wooden spoon through centre of each loaf. Sprinkle with flour. Cover and leave to rise in a warm place until double in size. Bake exactly as white bread.

Danish Loaves

Divide the risen dough into 3 equal portions and shape into oblongs. Put on to 1 or 2 large greased and floured baking trays. Dust with flour. Cover and leave to rise in the warm until double in size. With a sharp knife, cut a lengthwise split on each. Bake exactly as white bread.

Quick White Bread

Makes 2 small loaves

1 oz (25 g) fresh yeast
*¾ pt (425 ml) water (mix ⅔
cold with ⅓ boiling)*
*1 Vitamin C tablet of 25 mg,
crushed*
*1½ lb (675 g) plain white strong
flour*
2 level tsp salt
1 level tblsp caster sugar
1 oz (25 g) fat or 2 tblsp oil

This is a dough which, because of the inclusion of a small amount of Vitamin C (ascorbic acid), speeds up the whole process of bread making in that it does away with the need for two risings. Thus the ready-made dough may be shaped as soon as it is kneaded, left to rise *once only* and then baked. This method works better with fresh yeast than with dried and the quantity is usually increased; up to 1 oz (25 g) for 1½ lb (675 g) flour.

1. Well-grease 2 × 1-lb (450-g) oblong loaf tins with melted fat or oil. Dust with flour. Set aside for the time being.

2. Blend yeast smoothly with water then add crushed Vitamin C.

3. Sift flour and salt into a large bowl then toss in sugar. Rub in fat or make a well in the centre and pour in the oil.

4. Add the yeast liquid *in one go* then work to a dough with a fork or fingers. Draw together.

5. Turn out on to a floured surface and knead dough at least 10 minutes or until smooth, elastic and no longer sticky. If it stays very tacky, work in a little extra flour.

6. Divide in half and shape each piece to fit the prepared loaf tins. Cover with greased or oiled polythene and leave to rise in a warm place until double in size (about 50 minutes to 1 hour).

7. Dust lightly with flour or brush with egg and bake 30 to 35 minutes just above oven centre set to 450°F (230°C), Gas 8.

8. Turn out on to a wire cooling rack and turn the right way up. Leave until cold before storing in bread bin or freezing.

White Bread Variations

Makes 3

Flower Pot Loaves

These loaves have a delicious crusty crust and novel shape, and all the appeal and appearance of the best in homemade bread. But I have to qualify this by adding that the terracotta-coloured clay pots used more often for growing plants and flowers, must first be 'proved' as one 'proves' a new pan for omelettes to prevent the dough from sticking. This is how you go about it. For the amount of dough given in the Quick White Bread, thoroughly wash and dry 3 new clay flower pots, each measuring 5 inches (12.5 cm) across the top and 5 inches (12.5 cm) in height. Brush inside and out thickly with a bland-tasting salad oil such as corn or sunflower or, if preferred, spread inside and out with lard or white vegetable fat. Put into an oven which is empty, cooling down after baking scones or bread. Repeat 2 or 3 times, on separate occasions, so that the pots are well seasoned with oil or fat. *Do not wash.* Brush with grease again before using and, after loaves have been turned out, wipe out pots with a damp cloth. Smear insides lightly with oil or fat and dry off in the oven. One warning - do not use plastic pots or they will melt!

Shape risen dough into 3 balls and divide between the prepared pots. Cover with oiled or greased polythene or greaseproof paper, and leave to rise in a warm place until dough reaches tops of pots; about 50 minutes to 1 hour. Dust lightly with flour and then bake as Quick White Bread.

Norfolk Dumplings (1)

Makes 6

I often liken these to true Yorkshire pudding, since in the old days the dumplings were served as a first course with rich gravy from meat or game. Sometimes they are still served in this way but they are also eaten with stews, roasts and soups.

The dumplings can be made from one-third of the Quick White Bread or one-sixth of White Bread recipe. If using the first dough, shape into 6 dumplings, cover with greased polythene and leave to rise about 25 to 30 minutes in the warm until double in size. If using the second dough, allow it to rise first, shape into dumplings, cover as above and leave to rise again for about 20 to 25 minutes in the warm or until double in size. Simmer about

20 to 25 minutes in gently boiling water with a little added salt. Remove with a draining spoon and serve while very hot.

Makes 6

Norfolk Dumplings (2)
Sometimes called Thunder and Lightning, this is the sweet version of Norfolk Dumplings. Serve them hot as a sweet with whipped cream and black treacle.

Makes 3 large or 2 small loaves (depending on recipe used)

Bran Bread
To add fibre to white bread, allow 2 heaped tablespoons of fairly coarse bran to every 1 lb (450 g) flour, and toss into the dry ingredients with the sugar.

Makes 36 from White Bread or 18 from Quick White Bread

Assorted Rolls
If making rolls from White Bread recipe, leave dough to rise *first* before shaping, covering as bread and leaving to rise a second time for 25 to 30 minutes. If making rolls from Quick White Bread dough, shape straightaway, cover and then leave to rise 25 to 30 minutes. Bake at same temperature as given for bread, for 25 to 30 minutes. If using 2 trays, bake 1 on top shelf and 1 on shelf below

centre of oven, reversing trays at half time.

Plain Rolls

Makes 36 from White Bread or 18 from Quick White Bread

Shape dough into balls and put on to greased and floured baking trays. Cover, rise and bake. On removal from oven, brush immediately with water. When dry it glazes rolls.

Continental Rolls

Makes 36 from White Bread or 18 from Quick White Bread

Make exactly as Plain Rolls. Cut a cross on top of each. Brush with salted water. Cover, rise and bake.

Seed Rolls

Makes 36 from White Bread or 18 from Quick White Bread

Make as Plain Rolls. Brush with beaten eggs. Sprinkle with sesame, poppy or caraway seeds. Cover, rise and bake.

Vienna Rolls

Makes 36 from White Bread or 18 from Quick White Bread

Form dough into cigar-shaped oblongs then put on to greased and floured baking trays. Make 3 or 4 slashes with a sharp knife on top of each. Cover, rise and bake. Brush with water as soon as they come out of the oven for added crustiness.

Knot Rolls

Makes 36 from White Bread or 18 from Quick White Bread

Shape dough into 6 inch (15 cm) lengths and tie loosely into knots. Put on to greased and floured baking trays and brush with beaten egg. Cover, rise and bake.

Plait Rolls

Makes 36 from White Bread or 18 from Quick White Bread

Divide dough into 18 or 36 pieces then sub-divide pieces into 3. Form each into a 5-inch (12.5-cm) length and plait together. Place rolls on greased and floured baking trays. Brush with egg. Cover, rise and bake.

Almond Plait Rolls

Makes 36 from White Bread or 18 from Quick White Bread

Make as Plait Rolls. Brush with egg then sprinkle with flaked almonds, pressing them gently into dough with finger tips. Brush with melted butter or margarine and sprinkle lightly with paprika. Cover, rise and bake.

Hamburger Bun Rolls

Makes 36 from White Bread or 18 from Quick White Bread

Shape dough into rounds of ½ inch (1.25 cm) in thickness. Brush with egg. Cover, rise and bake.

Tip: All hamburger buns may, after brushing with egg, be sprinkled with sesame, poppy, caraway seeds or cracked wheat. They should then be covered, left to rise and baked as other rolls. For bigger buns, divide dough into 12 or 24 pieces and make the rounds larger in diameter.

Crown Loaf Rolls

Makes 36 from White Bread or 18 from Quick White Bread

Shape dough into balls. Put 5 round the inside edge of a greased 7-inch (17.5-cm) round cake tin and 1 in the middle. Brush with egg. Cover and leave to rise until rolls joint together. Bake as other rolls. Turn out of tin and ease apart to make domed, soft-sided rolls.

Salt Rolls

Makes 36 from White Bread or 18 from Quick White Bread

Shape dough into balls and put on to greased and floured baking trays. Brush with beaten egg. Sprinkle with coarse sea salt. Cover, rise and bake.

Onion 'Pretzels'

Makes 36 from White Bread or 18 from Quick White Bread

Shape dough into 5-inch (12.5-cm) lengths and form into rings by pinching ends together. Put on to greased and floured baking trays. Sprinkle with a little peeled and chopped onion and press into dough gently with fingertips. Brush with melted butter or margarine. Cover, rise and bake.

Pizza Base

Makes 6 or 12 from White Bread or 3 or 6 from Quick White Bread.

The full amount of risen White Bread dough will make the bases for 6 large or oblong Pizzas (13 × 9 inches or 32.5 × 22.5 cm) or 12 medium ones, each 9 inches (22.5 cm) in diameter. Unless you are bulk baking, I would suggest you use the recipe for Quick White Bread which makes half the number of pizzas. Spread the dough with toppings to taste (see general cook book), then leave Pizzas made from the risen and re-kneaded White Bread dough in the cool for ½ hour instead of a warm place. If making pizzas from Quick White Bread dough, leave to rise in the warm for 20 minutes then cover with selected toppings. Bake 30 minutes near top of oven set to 425°F (220°C), Gas 7.

Muffins

Enjoying a well-deserved revival, Muffins are quite easy to make and when toasted and buttered, are delicious for tea on a cold winter's day when something warm and fragrant is appreciated.

Take one-third of the risen White Bread dough or half the Quick White Bread dough. Roll out to about ½-inch (1.25-cm) thickness. Cut into 8 or 9 rounds with a 3½-inch (9-cm) biscuit cutter, re-rolling and re-cutting trimmings to make the full amount. Place on 2 well-greased and floured baking trays. Dust with flour. Cover and leave to rise until double in size. Bake 4 to 5 minutes 1 shelf above and 1 shelf below oven centre set to 450°F (230°C), Gas 8. Turn Muffins over then reverse position of trays. Continue to bake a further 4 to 5 minutes. Cool to lukewarm on a wire rack. Before serving, open up edges by pulling gently apart with fingers but *do not halve* at this stage. Toast on both sides either in an electric toaster or under the grill. Pull apart and spread the insides with butter. Serve straight away.

Blue Cheese and Walnut Bread

Makes 1 large loaf

Take one-third of risen White Bread dough or half of the Quick White Bread dough. Squeeze in 2 oz (50 g) chopped walnuts and 3 oz (75 g) crumbly blue cheese. Shape to fit a well-greased 2-lb (900-g) oblong loaf tin. Cover with greased polythene. Leave to rise in a warm place until dough reaches top of tin. Bake 40 to 45 minutes just above oven centre set to 400°F (200°C). Gas 6. Serve freshly sliced and buttered with soup, salad or egg dishes.

Dutch Cheese and Onion Bread

Makes 1 large loaf

Take one-third of the risen White Bread dough or half of the Quick White Bread dough. Squeeze in 2 oz (50 g) grated Edam cheese and 1 small chopped and lightly fried onion. Continue as previous loaf but before baking, brush with beaten egg and sprinkle with about 1 oz (25 g) extra grated Edam cheese. Slice and use as a base for open sandwiches or serve with cold meat or poultry salads.

Fruited Sugar Loaf

Makes 1 large loaf

Take one-third of risen White Bread dough or half of the Quick White Bread dough. Squeeze in 2 oz (50 g) *each* softened butter or margarine and light brown soft sugar, 4 oz (125 g) currants, 2 level tsp cinnamon and 1 level tsp finely grated orange peel. Continue as Blue Cheese and Walnut Bread but before baking, brush with beaten egg and sprinkle with about 1 oz (25 g) coarsely crushed cube sugar.

Makes 1 large cake

Lardy Cake

Take one-third of the risen White Bread dough and roll out into a strip of about ½ inch (1.25 cm) in thickness, making sure it is 3 times as long as it is wide (about 18 × 6 inches or 45 × 15 cm). Cover the top two-thirds with flakes of lard, using 1½ oz (40 g). Sprinkle with 1½ oz (40 g) caster sugar, 1 oz (25 g) sultanas and a little mixed spice. Fold in 3 like an envelope by bringing the bottom half (uncovered) to centre and folding top third over. Give the dough a quarter turn, re-roll into an oblong as before then once again add the same amount of lard, sugar, sultanas and spice to top two-thirds of the dough. Fold in 3, give dough a quarter turn then repeat the re-rolling and covering with lard, sugar, fruit and spice once more. Roll out to fit a 10 × 8-inch (25 × 20-cm) well-greased roasting tin. Cover. Leave to rise for 1 hour in a warm place.

Bake about 40 minutes just above oven centre set to 425°F (220°C), Gas 7. Leave in the tin until all the fat has been absorbed by the cake then invert on to a wire cooling rack. Serve upside down so that the syrupy base shows. Eat freshly made with butter.

Milk Bread (Plain)

Makes 2 large or 3 small loaves

Follow recipe for White Bread or Quick White Bread but use half warm milk and half warm water for mixing. If preferred, use all milk but allow a little longer for the dough to rise. The texture of the bread will be marginally less light than if made with all water, and the crust will be noticeably darker. Any of the previous recipes may be made with the Milk Bread dough.

Malt Bread

Makes 2 loaves

3 oz (75 g) malt extract
2 level tblsp black treacle
1 oz (25 g) butter
1 lb (450 g) plain white strong
*   flour*
1 level tsp salt
8 oz (225 g) sultanas or seedless
*   raisins*
1 oz (25 g) fresh yeast
¼ pt (150 ml) warm water
*   PLUS 3 extra tblsp*

1. Put first 3 ingredients in a saucepan and stand over a low heat until melted. Cool to lukewarm.

2. Sift flour and salt into a bowl. Toss in sultanas or raisins.

3. Mix yeast smoothly with a little water then add remainder.

4. Add yeast liquid to dry ingredients with melted mixture. Work to a dough. Turn out on to a floured surface and knead for 10 to 15 minutes or until dough is smooth, elastic and no longer sticky.

5. Shape to fit 2 × 1-lb (450-g) well greased and floured oblong loaf tins. Cover with greased polythene.

6. Leave to rise in the warm until light, puffy and double in size; about 1 to 1¼ hours.

7. Brush lightly with milk. Bake 45 minutes just above oven centre set to 400°F (200°C), Gas 6. Cool on a wire rack and serve sliced and buttered.

MILK BREADS

This is a slightly enriched version of the basic white bread dough, resulting in bread and rolls with a more 'cakey' texture. In general, they will have a softer and darker crust. Any milk can be used, but those people who have to watch their fat intake will obviously prefer to use low fat skimmed. Other choices can be ordinary bottled milk, long life milk or canned evaporated milk, diluted as directed.

Milk Bread

Makes 3 large loaves

½ oz or 15 g (1 level tblsp) dried
   yeast with 2 level tsp caster
   sugar, honey or syrup OR
   1 oz (25 g) fresh yeast and no
   sugar
¾ pt (425 ml) EACH warm
   milk and warm water (mix
   ²⁄₃ cold with ¹⁄₃ boiling)
3 lb (1.35 kg) plain white
   strong flour
4 level tsp salt
1 level tblsp caster sugar
6 oz (175 g) margarine, butter,
   lard or white cooking fat (or
   mixture of any of these)

1. Well grease 3 oblong loaf tins, each 2 lb or 900 g. Set aside.

2. Mix dried yeast with sugar, honey or syrup then add half the liquid. Leave in a warm place for about 10 to 15 minutes or until mixture foams up. Alternatively, blend liquid gradually into the fresh yeast.

3. Sift flour and salt into a bowl. Toss in sugar then rub in fat finely.

4. Add yeast liquid, and remaining milk and water, *in one go* then draw together to a dough with fork or fingertips.

5. Turn out on to a floured surface and knead a good 10 minutes or until dough is smooth, elastic and no longer sticky. If necessary, work in extra flour.

6. Shape into a ball and put into a greased or oiled bowl. Cover with greased or oiled plate and leave to rise until double in size. (See points 7 and 8 of Basic Techniques).

41

7. Turn out on to a floured surface and knead briefly until smooth, elastic and no longer sticky.

8. Divide equally into 3 pieces and shape to fit prepared tins. Brush tops with beaten egg or milk, cover with oiled or greased polythene and leave to rise in a warm place for ¾ to 1 hour or until light, puffy and at least double in size.

9. Bake 50 to 55 minutes just above oven centre set to 400°F (200°C), Gas 6. If tins are unable to sit on one shelf, bake 2 above oven centre and 1 below, changing round at half time.

10. Leave in tins for 5 minutes then tap out on to wire cooling racks.

11. For extra crusty sides, remove loaves from oven 5 minutes early. Tap out on to a greased baking tray, turn the right way up and crispen in the oven for an extra 10 minutes.

12. Cool completely on wire racks before storing in bread bins or freezing.

Bap Loaves

Makes 6

Divide the Milk Bread dough into 6 equal pieces, knead lightly then pat each into a round of ½ inch (1.25 cm) in thickness. Put on to 3 large greased and floured trays. Cover. Leave to rise in a warm place until loaves are light, puffy and double in size (about 45 minutes). Dust with flour and press down centres of each with the back of a wooden spoon. Bake at same temperature as large loaves, allowing 25 minutes. Use 3 shelves in the oven, but reverse top and bottom trays at half time. Slip Baps on to wire cooling racks and cover with clean tea towels to ensure soft crusts. Remove towels when loaves are cold.

Bap Rolls

Makes 36

Make exactly as Bap Loaves but shape risen dough into 36 rounds of ½ inch (1.25 cm) in thickness. Put on to greased and floured trays. Cover. Leave to rise about 35 minutes in the warm or until rolls are light, puffy and double in size. Dust with flour. Bake 15 minutes in hot oven set to 400°F (200°C), Gas 6. Transfer to cooling racks. Cover as Bap Loaves. Remove towels when rolls are cold.

Bridge Rolls

Makes 36

Lightly knead risen Milk Bread dough then divide into 36 pieces and roll each into a 5-inch (12.5-cm) 'cigar' shape. Put close together on to large greased and floured baking trays. Cover. Leave to rise about 30 minutes in a warm place when rolls should puff up and join together. Brush with beaten egg and bake as directed for Bap Rolls. Cool for a few minutes then break gently apart. Slip on to wire racks and leave until completely cold before splitting and serving with butter, or filling as sandwiches.

Party Bridge Rolls

Makes 72

Make as Bridge Rolls above but shape dough into 'cigars' half the size.

Fruit Bread

Makes 1 loaf

Take one-third of risen Milk Bread dough and squeeze into it about 4 to 6 oz (125 to 175 g) mixed dried fruit. Shape to fit a well greased 2-lb (900-g) oblong loaf tin. Cover and leave to rise about 50 minutes in the warm when loaf should be light, puffy and double in size. Brush with beaten egg and bake about 50 minutes just above oven centre set to 400°F (200°C), Gas 6. Turn out and cool on a wire rack. Serve sliced and buttered.

Plaits

Makes 3 loaves

Divide risen and lightly kneaded Milk Bread dough into 3 then sub-divide each into a further 3 pieces. Roll into 16-inch (40-cm) lengths. Plait together in threes to make 3 loaves. Put, side by side, on to a *large* greased and floured baking tray. Cover. Leave in a warm place to rise, allowing about 45 to 50 minutes. Brush with beaten egg then bake as for Bap Loaves. Cool on wire racks.

Selkirk Bannock

Makes 1 cake

A Scottish New Year speciality. Take off one-sixth of the risen Milk Bread dough and knead into it 3 oz (75 g) mixed dried fruit and 1 oz (25 g) caster sugar. Shape into an 8-inch (20-cm) round and put on to a greased and floured baking tray. Brush with milk. Cover. Leave to rise in a warm place for 30 to 40 minutes or until light, puffy and double in size. Bake until golden brown, allowing 25 minutes just above oven centre set to 375°F (190°C), Gas 5. Cool on a wire rack.

Makes 5

Yorkshire Tea Cakes

Take one-third of risen Milk Bread dough, knead lightly then divide into 5 equal pieces. Shape into ½-inch (1.25-cm) thick rounds. Place, with gaps between, on to 2 large greased and floured baking trays. Brush tops with milk. Cover. Leave in a warm place to rise for about 50 minutes when Tea Cakes should be light, puffy and twice their original size. Bake 15 minutes on 1 shelf above and 1 shelf below oven centre set to 425°F (220°C), Gas 7, reversing position of trays at half time. Cool on a wire rack. Serve split and buttered. Alternatively, split and toast before buttering.

Makes 5

Fruited Yorkshire Tea Cakes

Make exactly as above but knead 2 oz (50 g) currants into the risen dough.

BUNS

Welcome always, here are some traditional bun recipes which take you through from ordinary sweet round buns to the slightly more elaborate Spice, Fruit, Hot Cross, Bath, Swiss and Chelsea. Not even Cornish Splits have been missed, so what better excuse for indulging in clotted cream and raspberry or strawberry jam!

Plain Buns

Makes 8

2 level tsp dried yeast with 1
    level tsp caster sugar, honey
    or syrup OR ½ oz (15 g) fresh
    yeast and no sugar
¼ pt (150 ml) warm milk
8 oz (225 g) plain white strong
    flour
½ level tsp salt
½ level tsp caster sugar
1 oz (25 g) butter or margarine

1. Mix dried yeast with sugar, honey or syrup then add milk. Leave in a warm place for 10 to 15 minutes or until mixture foams up. Alternatively, blend fresh yeast with milk until smooth.

2. Sift flour and salt into a bowl. Toss in sugar. Rub in butter or margarine.

3. Add yeast liquid *in one go* then draw together with fork or fingertips. Turn out on to floured surface and knead a good 10 minutes or until dough is smooth, elastic and no longer sticky.

4. Shape into ball, put into greased bowl and cover with a greased plate. Leave 1 hour to rise until double in size.

5. Turn out on to floured surface and knead lightly until smooth. Shape into 8 round buns. Place on greased and floured baking tray. Cover. Leave to rise in the warm until light, puffy and double in size (about ½ hour).

6. Brush with beaten egg and bake 15 minutes just above oven centre set to 425°F (220°C), Gas 7, until well risen and golden brown. Cool on a wire rack.

Makes 8

Sticky Buns
As soon as buns have been removed to a wire cooling rack, brush with honey or syrup. Alternatively, brush with glaze made as follows: dissolve 1½ oz (40 g) granulated sugar in 2 tblsp *each* of milk and water. Bring to boil and boil about 5 minutes or until glaze thickens slightly and looks syrupy.

Makes 8

Spice Buns
Make exactly as Plain Buns, but sift flour and salt with 2 level teaspoons mixed spice.

Makes 8

Fruit Buns
Make exactly as Spice Buns but add 1½ oz (40 g) caster sugar and 4 oz (125 g) mixed dried fruit after rubbing in the fat.

Hot Cross Buns

Make exactly as for Plain Buns but sift flour and salt with 2 level teaspoons mixed spice. Increase sugar to 1½ oz (40 g). Toss in 4 oz (125 g) mixed dried fruit after rubbing in fat. Shape into 8 buns, put on to greased and floured baking tray and top each with a cross made from shortcrust pastry. While still hot, brush with glaze as given for Sticky Buns or, if preferred, use syrup or honey.

Bath Buns

Make exactly as Plain Buns but sift flour and salt with 1½ level teaspoons mixed spice. Increase sugar to 1½ oz (40 g). Toss in 2 oz (50 g) currants and 1 oz (25 g) mixed chopped peel after rubbing in fat. Add 1 beaten egg (Grade- 3) with yeast liquid to form a soft dough. Beat thoroughly in bowl. Cover with an oiled or greased plate and leave to rise for about 1 hour or until double in size. Beat again for about 1 minute then spoon 12 mounds of dough on to 2 greased and floured baking trays. Cover. Leave to rise in the warm for about 30 minutes or until light, puffy and double in size. Brush with egg then sprinkle lightly with coarsely crushed cube sugar. Bake as Plain Buns, placing trays 1 shelf above and 1 shelf below oven centre. Change trays round at half time. Cool on a wire rack.

Makes 8

Swiss Buns

Make exactly as Plain Buns but divide risen dough into 8 pieces and form into 5-inch (12.5-cm) 'cigar' shapes instead of round buns. When cold, cover tops with a thickish glacé icing made by mixing 4 oz (125 g) sifted icing sugar with 4 to 5 teaspoons warm water. If liked, flavour icing with ½ teaspoon vanilla essence and colour pale pink with food colouring.

Makes 8

Cornish Splits

Make exactly as Plain Buns. When cold, cut in half and fill generously with clotted cream and raspberry or strawberry jam. Dust tops with sifted icing sugar.

Makes 9

Chelsea Buns

Make dough exactly as for Plain Buns. After dough has risen, knead until smooth then roll into a 12 × 9-inch (30 × 23-cm) rectangle. Spread with 1 oz (25 g) melted butter then sprinkle

51

with 4 oz (125 g) mixed dried fruit and 2 oz (50 g) light brown soft sugar. Roll up like a Swiss roll, starting from one of the longer sides. Cut into 9 slices. Place close together in a single layer in a well-greased 7-inch (17.5-cm) square cake tin. Cover. Leave to rise in a warm place until buns have doubled in size and join together. Allow about 50 minutes. Bake 25 minutes just above oven centre set to 425°F (220°C), Gas 7. Turn out on to a wire cooling rack and ease gently apart when cold. Eat freshly made.

CAKES & PASTRIES

Not all cakes and pastries are made by rubbing-in, creaming, whisking and melting, and here you will discover a generous yeasted variety to include a fruited Christmas Garland, German Stollen, Danish Pastries, Croissants, a mixed batch of Doughnuts and a mouth-watering Crumble Cake.

Swedish Tea Cake

Serves 8 to 10

Yeast 'sponge'
2 level tsp dried yeast with ½
  level tsp caster sugar,
  honey or syrup OR ½ oz
  (15 g) fresh yeast and ½ level
  tsp caster sugar
4½ tblsp warm milk
2 oz (50 g) plain white strong
  flour

Remaining ingredients
6 oz (175 g) plain white strong
  flour
½ level tsp salt
1 oz (25 g) caster sugar

1. Mix dried yeast with sugar, honey or syrup then add the milk. Leave to stand in the warm for 5 minutes. Stir in the flour. Leave in the warm for a further 20 minutes or until frothy. If using fresh yeast stir, with ½ teaspoon sugar, into milk. Add flour and leave in the warm for 20 minutes or until it, too, froths up and looks like beer with a head.

2. Meanwhile sift flour, salt and sugar into a bowl. Rub in butter or margarine. Toss in cardamom then add yeast liquid and egg *in one go*. Using a fork or fingers, mix to a soft dough.

3. Turn out on to a floured surface and knead a good 10 minutes or until smooth, elastic and no longer sticky. If necessary, work in a little extra flour.

4. Shape into a ball, put into an oiled or greased bowl and cover with a greased plate. Leave to rise until double in size. (For rising times, see points 7 and 8 of Basic Techniques.)

1 oz (25 g) butter or margarine
crushed seeds from 8
  cardamom pods
1 Grade 3 egg, beaten

Filling
3 oz (75 g) softened butter
3 oz (75 g) light brown soft
  sugar
1½ rounded tsp cinnamon

Topping
beaten egg
about 1 oz (25 g) flaked
  almonds

5. Turn out on to a floured surface and knead lightly until smooth. Roll into a 14 × 12-inch (35 × 30-cm) rectangle. Spread with butter then sprinkle with sugar and cinnamon.

6. Roll up like a Swiss roll, starting from one of the longer sides, then place diagonally on to a greased and floured baking tray with join underneath. Cover and leave to rise in a warm place for about 45 minutes to 1 hour or until double in size.

7. Brush with beaten egg, sprinkle with almonds and bake until golden brown and well risen; about 35 to 40 minutes in oven set to 375°F (190°C), Gas 5. Cool on a wire rack. Serve fresh.

Swedish Horseshoe Cake

Make as Swedish Tea Cake but curve roll into a horseshoe on a
greased and floured baking tray. Serve fresh.

Swedish Christmas Kranz (Garland)

Make as Swedish Tea Cake but curve roll into a ring on baking
tray and pinch edges together to join. Do not brush with egg and
omit almonds. When cold, spread with glacé icing as given in
recipe under Swiss Buns (page 51). Make double quantity and
leave white. When set, decorate with green glacé cherries and
silver and gold balls. Attach a bright bow of red ribbon at the
point where the ring meets, holding it in place with extra icing.

Filling Variation

To change the filling, spread dough with butter then cover with
4 to 6 oz (125 to 175 g) stiff almond paste, coarsely grated.

Crumble Cake

Make up the dough as given for Swedish Tea Cake but omit
cardamom. After dough has risen and been kneaded for the

second time, press into a 7-inch (17.5-cm) well greased square cake tin. Brush with 2 level tablespoons melted jam, flavour to taste (apricot is excellent). For the crumble, sift 1 oz (25 g) plain flour and ½ level teaspoon cinnamon into a bowl then rub in ½ oz (15 g) butter or margarine. Toss in ½ oz (15 g) caster sugar. Sprinkle over the jam. Cover. Leave to rise 45 minutes to 1 hour or until cake is double in size and is light and puffy. Bake as Swedish Tea Cake for about 45 minutes to 1 hour in oven centre set to 375°F (190°C), Gas 5. When ready, cake should be well-risen and golden brown. To test, push a metal skewer gently into centre. If it comes out clean and dry, the cake is done. If not, return to oven for a further 5 to 10 minutes.

Serves 8 to 10

Stollen
This is a German Christmas cake, usually eaten over the whole of the festive season. It is served sliced and buttered.

Make up dough as given for Swedish Tea Cake, omitting cardamom. After dough has risen, knead into it 1 oz (25 g) flaked and slivered almonds, 1 level teaspoon finely grated lemon peel, 4 oz (125 g) sultanas and 2 oz (50 g) mixed chopped peel. Roll out into a 10-inch (25-cm) round and spread with 2 oz (50 g) softened butter. Fold dough in 3 as you would fold an omelette then pinch joins lightly together. Put on to a greased and floured baking tray with join on top. Cover. Leave to rise for 30 to 40 minutes or until double in size and puffy. Brush with 1 oz (25 g) melted butter and bake 35 to 40 minutes just above oven centre set to 400°F (200°C), Gas 6. Cool on a wire rack and dust thickly with sifted icing sugar while still lukewarm. Store in an airtight tin.

Makes 16

Danish Pastries

Known as *Wienerbrot* (Viennese Bread) in Scandinavia and Northern Europe, Danish Pastries can appear in all shapes and sizes from windmills to crescents. I shall keep to one type only (the easiest!), with a filling of almond paste.

Make up dough as given for Swedish Tea Cake but omit cardamom. Leave to rise and knead until smooth. Roll out into a rectangle measuring 18 × 6 inches (45 × 15 cm). Cover top two-thirds with dabs of butter, allowing 2 oz or 50 g. Fold in 3 like an envelope by bringing bottom third to centre and folding top third over. Seal open edges by pressing with a rolling pin.

Refrigerate 15 minutes. Give dough a quarter turn then repeat the rolling, buttering, folding, sealing edges and turning twice more, using a total of 6 oz (175 g) butter. Transfer to a buttered and floured plate, cover with buttered paper and refrigerate 30 minutes. Turn out on to a flour-dusted surface and roll out into a 16-inch (40-cm) square. Cut into 16 squares and put a piece of almond paste on to the centre of each, using a total amount of 4 oz (125 g). Dampen edges with water then fold over to form triangles. Press edges well together to seal. Transfer pastries to well buttered and lightly floured baking trays. Cover. Leave to rise in the warm for about 45 minutes or until light, puffy and double in size. Bake about 15 minutes 1 shelf above and 1 shelf below oven centre set to 425°F (220°C), Gas 7, reversing position of trays at half time. Pastries are ready when they are well-risen and golden brown. Transfer to a wire cooling rack and brush tops thickly with melted and sieved apricot jam then sprinkle with lightly toasted almond flakes.

Croissants, Easy Style

Make exactly as Danish Pastries but roll refrigerated pastry into an oblong measuring 18 × 6 inches (45 × 15 cm). Cut into 3 × 6-inch (15-cm) squares then cut each square into 2 triangles. Brush with half a small beaten egg, mixed with a pinch of sugar, then roll up from the widest part to the pointed end. Put croissants on to a greased and floured baking tray, curving them as you do it. Cover. Leave to rise in the warm for about 40 minutes or until double in size, light and puffy. Brush with beaten egg then bake 15 to 20 minutes just above oven centre set to 425°F (220°C), Gas 7. Cool on a wire rack but eat while still warm.

Doughnuts

Make dough exactly as given for Swedish Tea Cake, omitting cardamom. After first rising, knead lightly and divide into 12 pieces. Shape each into a ball. Cover. Leave to rise in the warm for for about 30 minutes or until light, puffy and double in size. Lower, a few at a time, into a deep pan half-filled with melted hot fat or oil (temperature 350°F or 180°C) and fry about 7 to 10 minutes, turning frequently until golden brown and well-risen. Drain on crumpled kitchen paper and toss in caster sugar.

Makes 12

Jam Doughnuts

Make as Doughnuts. After coating with sugar, make incision in each with a knife and spoon in a little jam. Alternatively, pipe some melted and sieved plum jam into incisions.

Makes 12

Cream Doughnuts

Split each Doughnut two-thirds of the way through then fill with sweetened whipped cream. If liked, add some jam as well.

Makes 20

Doughnut Rings

Make dough exactly as given for Swedish Tea Cake, omitting cardamom. After first rising, knead lightly then roll out to ½ inch (1.25 cm) in thickness. Cut into rounds with a 3-inch (7.5-cm) biscuit cutter then remove centres with 1½-inch (3- to 4-cm) cutter. Re-roll and re-cut centres to make more doughnuts. Cover. Leave to rise in the warm for about 25 to 30 minutes until light, puffy and double in size. Fry, a few at a time, for about 7 minutes in a deep pan half-filled with hot fat or oil (temperature 350°F or 180°C). Drain on crumpled kitchen paper then toss in about 1½ oz (40 g) caster sugar mixed with 1 level teaspoon cinnamon.

Makes 12

Doughnut Splits
Make as plain Doughnuts but shape dough into 5- or 6-inch (12.5- or 15-cm) lengths instead of rounds. Fry and toss in caster sugar as directed in recipe for Doughnuts. When cold, split lengthwise and pipe in sweetened whipped cream.

BROWN BREADS

Gathering popularity almost by the minute, I have put together a short selection of basic bread and rolls to please all those who love the taste, texture and goodness of brown flour. Brown Pizza is, in my estimation, tastier than white and I hope the Granary Bread, for which I have had so many requests in recent years, will be as appreciated in your home as it is in mine.

Quick Brown Bread

Makes 1 loaf

2 level tsp dried yeast with 1
  level tsp caster sugar, honey
  or syrup OR ½ oz (15 g) fresh
  yeast and no sugar
½ pt (275 ml) warm water (mix
  ⅔ cold with ⅓ boiling)
1 lb (450 g) brown flour
1½ level tsp salt
½ oz (15 g) margarine or white
  vegetable cooking fat

1. Stir dried yeast and sugar, honey or syrup into water. Leave to stand about 20 minutes in a warm place or until mixture froths up. Alternatively, blend fresh yeast smoothly with the water.

2. Tip flour into a bowl. Toss in salt then rub in margarine or fat with fingertips. Add yeast liquid to flour *in one go* and mix to a dough with a fork or fingertips. Knead until smooth, elastic and no longer sticky (10 to 15 minutes).

3. Shape to fit a 2 lb (900 g) well greased and lightly floured oblong loaf tin. Cover with greased or oiled polythene or greaseproof paper. Leave to rise until double in size (about ¾ to 1 hour in a warm place; 1¼ to 1½ hours at kitchen temperature; 1½ to 2 hours in the cool).

4. Brush with salt water then leave plain or sprinkle with cracked wheat. Bake 45 to 50 minutes just above oven centre set to 450°F (230°C), Gas 8. Cool on a wire rack.

Cob Loaves

Make dough as given for Quick Brown Bread then divide into 2 pieces. Shape each into a round ball. Put on to a large greased and floured baking tray. Flatten a little with your hand. Cover and leave to rise as directed in previous recipe. Cut a cross on top of each with a knife, then bake about 35 to 40 minutes just above oven centre set to 450°F (230°C), Gas 8. Cool on a wire rack before putting into bread bin or freezing.

Brown Pizza

Use half quantity of Quick Brown Bread dough for a large Pizza base, following instructions for Pizza made with white dough (page 34).

Spread with a tomato topping. Cover and leave to rise in a warm place until light, puffy and double in size. Add rest of chosen ingredients to Pizza. Bake 30 minutes just above oven centre set to 425°F (220°C), Gas 7. Serve hot. Serves 2 to 4 depending on whether Pizza is to be a starter, main course or snack.

Makes 1

Brown Bran Bread

Follow recipe for Quick Brown Bread but use half white and half brown flour and 3 heaped tablespoons coarse bran.

Makes 12

Brown Sesame Rolls

Follow recipe for Quick Brown Bread. Divide dough into 12 pieces and shape into balls. Put on to a greased and floured baking tray. Cover. Leave to rise until light, puffy and double in size. Brush with salted water then sprinkle with sesame seeds. Bake 10 to 15 minutes near top of oven set to 450°F (230°C), Gas 8. Cool on a wire rack.

Makes 12

Brown Clover Leaf Rolls

Follow recipe for Quick Brown Bread then divide dough equally into 36 pieces and form into small balls. Drop, in groups of 3, into well-greased bun tins to form clover leaf shapes. Cover. Leave to rise until light, puffy and double in size. Brush with beaten egg or salted water. Bake as Brown Sesame Rolls. Cool on a wire rack.

Makes 1 loaf

Granary Bread
Follow recipe for Quick Brown Bread using half plain white strong flour and half granary meal (granary flour).

Makes 3 loaves

Brown Bread (Traditional)
Make exactly as White Bread (page 22) but use 2 lb (900 g) brown flour and 1 lb (450 g) plain white strong flour.

Makes 3 loaves

Wholemeal or Wholewheat Bread
Make exactly as White Bread (page 22), but use 3 lb (1.35 kg) wholemeal or wholewheat flour and double the amount of yeast. Allow extra time for rising; a minimum of 30 minutes.

SPECIALITIES

These are yeasted specialities from home and abroad – 'collectors pieces', as I call them, gathered during my many years of travelling. Some, like Crumpets, come from home territory while Blinis stem from Russia, Brioches from France and Rye Bread from Scandinavia. For those who want a taste of ethnic cooking, there are also Jewish Bagels and Chollah, Indian breads and Balkan Pitta.

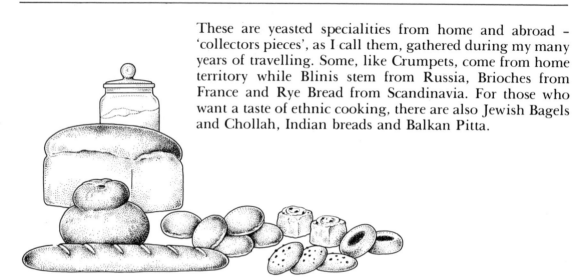

Crumpets

Makes about 18

2 level tsp dried yeast with 1
  level tsp caster sugar, honey
  or syrup OR ½ oz (15 g) fresh
  yeast and ½ level tsp caster
  sugar
½ pt (275 ml) warm water (mix ⅔
  cold with ⅓ boiling)
12 oz (350 g) plain white strong
  flour
½ level tsp bicarbonate of soda
1 level tsp salt
7 fl. oz (200 ml) warm milk
  (mix ⅔ cold with ⅓
  boiling)

1. Lightly grease a clean griddle or *large* frying pan, also insides of 4 × 3-inch (7.5-cm) plain metal biscuit cutters.

2. Stir dried yeast and sugar, honey or syrup into water. Leave to stand 5 minutes. Mix in *half* the flour and stir well. Alternatively, mix fresh yeast and sugar with water then add *half* the flour and beat well. Leave either brew in a warm place for about 30 to 40 minutes or until light and frothy.

3. Gradually add rest of ingredients and beat until smooth. The consistency should be that of a pouring batter so, if necessary, add a little extra warm milk.

4. Heat griddle or pan until a few drops of water, sprinkled on to the surface, bounce off. Stand biscuit cutters in pan and pour 2 tblsp batter into each. Cook until undersides set and holes burst on top. Remove rings then turn crumpets over. Fry until golden brown. Cool on wire rack. Repeat with rest of batter. Serve, toasted and spread with butter.

Blinis or Russian Pancakes

Makes 15 to 16

8 oz (225 g) plain white strong
  flour
½ level tsp salt
2 level tsp caster sugar
2 level tsp dried yeast OR ½ oz
  (15 g) fresh yeast
½ pt (275 ml) warm milk
  (mix. ⅔ cold with ⅓
  boiling)
1 Grade 3 egg, separated
Oil for frying

A wonderful and unusual main course, each pancake is served coated with melted butter and accompanied by separate bowls and plates of soured cream, smoked salmon and caviar (the mock lumpfish caviar from Scandinavia or Germany in the absence of the real thing!).

1. Sift flour and salt into a bowl then toss in sugar. Mix in dried yeast or crumble in the fresh yeast.

2. Stir in the milk. Cover. Leave to rise until well-frothed in a warm place, allowing 30 to 40 minutes.

3. Add egg yolk and stir batter well to mix. Fold in egg white, beaten to a stiff snow.

4. Well grease a heavy-based frying pan. Heat until hot. Spread heaped tablespoons of batter over the centre. Fry until underside is golden. Turn over and continue to fry until second side is golden. Remove from pan on to a clean tea towel.

5. Stack 1 on top of the other as Blinis are cooked to keep warm. Serve straight away with the suggested accompaniments.

Makes 15 to 16

Sweet Blinis
Prepare exactly as previous Blinis but spoon melted butter over each pancake then serve warm with either thick whipped cream or vanilla ice cream.

Makes 15 to 16

Honey Blinis
Prepare exactly as Blinis but spread fairly thickly with honey, coat with a little melted butter then top each with 1 tablespoon vanilla ice cream and sprinkle with finely chopped walnuts.

Brioches

Makes 12

Yeast 'sponge'
2 *level tsp dried yeast OR ½ oz (15 g) fresh yeast*
3 *tblsp warm milk*
1 *level tsp caster sugar*
1 *oz (25 g) plain white strong flour*

Remaining ingredients
8 *oz (225 g) plain white strong flour*
¼ *level tsp salt*
½ *oz (15 g) caster sugar*
2 *oz (50 g) butter*
2 *Grade 3 eggs, beaten*

Topping
Extra beaten egg

1. To make yeast 'sponge', blend all ingredients well together and cover. Leave in a warm place to rise for 20 to 30 minutes or until frothy.

2. Sift flour and salt into a bowl. Toss in sugar then rub in butter.

3. Mix to a soft dough with yeast liquid and beaten eggs.

4. Draw together then knead on a floured surface 10 to 15 minutes or until smooth, elastic and no longer sticky. Work in a little extra flour if dough remains on the tacky side.

5. Put into an oiled bowl. Cover with an oiled plate and leave to to rise until double in size.

6. Knead quickly on a floured surface then divide three-quarters of the dough into 12 pieces. Shape into balls and drop into well-buttered fluted brioche tins or deep bun tins. Brush with egg.

7. Roll remaining dough into 12 small balls and place on top of

Brioches. Hold in place by pushing a flour-dusted handle of a slim wooden spoon through each.

8. Cover. Leave to rise 30 to 40 minutes in a warm place or until light, puffy and double in size.

9. Brush with more egg and bake until a deep gold; about 8 to 10 minutes just above oven centre set to 450°F (230°C), Gas 8.

10. Cool on a wire rack and serve at breakfast time with butter and jam.

Makes 12

Novelty Brioches
Make as for Brioche, brush with egg and then sprinkle with fairly well-crushed cube sugar before baking. Serve with butter and jam.

Naan Bread

Makes 6

*2 level tsp dried yeast with 1
    level tsp caster sugar, honey or
    syrup OR ½ oz (15 g) fresh
    yeast and no sugar*
7 fl. oz (200 ml) warm milk
*1 lb (450 g) plain white strong
    flour*
½ level tsp salt
1 level tsp baking powder
2 level tsp caster sugar
1 Grade 3 egg, well beaten
2 tblsp corn or peanut oil
4 level tblsp natural yogurt

This is Indian bread, traditionally served with Tandoori dishes
and Westernised barbecued foods. It is usually cooked under a grill
and needs at least 4 inches (10 cm) space between the grill pan and
the source of heat to give the bread a chance to puff up without
catching alight.

1. Stir dried yeast and sugar, honey or syrup into milk and leave
in the warm for 20 to 30 minutes or until frothy. Alternatively,
blend fresh yeast smoothly with milk.

2. Sift flour, salt and baking powder into a bowl. Toss in sugar.
Mix to dough with yeast liquid, egg, oil and yogurt. Draw
together with fork or fingertips.

3. Turn on to floured surface and knead about 10 to 15 minutes or
until smooth, elastic and no longer sticky. Shape into a ball and
put into an oiled bowl. Cover with a greased plate and leave to rise
until double in size. (For rising times, see points 7 and 8 of Basic
Techniques.)

4. Turn out on to a floured surface and re-knead until smooth. Divide into 6 pieces and shape each into an oval measuring 10×4 inches (25×10 cm).

5. Stand, 3 at a time, in grill pan and brush with water. Grill 2 to 3 minutes or until puffy and light brown. Turn over.

6. Brush with more water and grill second sides for another 2 to 3 minutes. Serve straight away.

Tip: If Naan Bread is made ahead of time, it can be re-heated on a barbecue grid.

Chollah

Makes 2

*2 level tsp dried yeast with 1
level tsp caster sugar, honey
or syrup OR ½ oz (15 g) fresh
yeast and no sugar*

*8 fl. oz (225 ml) warm water
(mix ⅔ cold with ⅓
boiling)*

*1 lb (450 g) plain white strong
flour*

1 level tsp salt

1 extra level tblsp caster sugar

*2 tblsp salad oil or 2 tblsp
melted vegetable margarine*

1 Grade 3 egg, beaten

This is Jewish Sabbath bread, always plaited so that it can be easily divided without being cut. The traditional 4-strand plaiting is not that easy to do, so I have settled for the more manageable 3-strand plait. As the Jewish food laws prohibit meat and milk from being eaten together, the Chollah is made with water and either oil or melted vegetable margarine; no milk or butter have been included.

1. Stir dried yeast and sugar, honey or syrup into the water. Leave in a warm place for 20 to 30 minutes or until mixture froths up and looks like a glass of foaming beer. Alternatively, blend fresh yeast smoothly with water.

2. Sift flour and salt into a bowl. Toss in sugar. Mix to a softish dough with yeast liquid, oil or margarine and the beaten egg.

3. Turn out on to a floured surface and knead lightly for 10 to 15 minutes or until dough is smooth, elastic and no longer sticky. Work in a little extra flour if the mixture seems on the tacky side.

4. Shape into a ball and put into an oiled bowl. Cover with an oiled plate and leave to rise until double in size. (For rising times, see points 7 and 8 of Basic Techniques.)

5. Turn out on to a floured surface and knead briefly until smooth. Divide into 2 equal-sized pieces.

6. Sub-divide both pieces into 3 and roll each into a 16-inch (40-cm) length. Plait together. Repeat with second piece of dough to make 2 Chollahs.

7. Put on to a large greased and floured baking tray. Cover and leave to rise in the warm for about 45 to 50 minutes or until loaves are light, puffy and double in size.

8. Brush with extra beaten egg and bake 30 to 40 minutes just above oven centre set to 400°F (200°C), Gas 6. When ready, the loaves should be a warm golden brown. Cool on a wire rack.

Plain Chollah

If preferred, omit egg and use ½ pt (275 ml) water. To make Poppy Seed Chollah, brush with egg and sprinkle with poppy seeds.

Bagels

These Jewish style rolls are shaped into rings and served split and buttered – they are especially good with cream cheese and smoked fish.

Make up Chollah dough. After first rising, re-knead until smooth then divide into 20 equal pieces. Roll each into a 7-inch (17.5-cm) length. Curve into a ring and pinch edges well together to seal. Place on floured board and leave to stand in the warm for 15 minutes. Afterwards poach individually, in boiling salted water, for about ¼ minute. Remove from water with a slotted spoon, then transfer to 2 greased and lightly floured baking trays. Brush with beaten egg. Bake 1 shelf above and 1 shelf below oven centre set to 400°F (200°C), Gas 6. Allow 10 to 15 minutes or until golden and crusty, reversing position of trays at half time. Cool on a wire rack. Eat freshly made if possible. Store in an airtight container when cold.

French Sticks

Makes 2

2 level tsp dried yeast and 1
  level tsp caster sugar, honey
  or syrup OR ½ oz (15 g) fresh
  yeast and no sugar
½ pt (275 ml) warm water (mix
  ⅔ cold with ⅓ boiling)
1 Vitamin C tablet of 25 mg,
  crushed
1 lb (450 g) plain white strong
  flour
1 level tsp salt

1. Stir dried yeast and sugar, honey or syrup into the water. Leave in the warm for 20 to 30 minutes or until frothy. Or blend fresh yeast with water. Stir Vitamin C into either mixture.

2. Sift flour and salt into a bowl. Mix to a dough with yeast liquid then turn out on to floured surface. Knead for 10 to 15 minutes or until smooth, elastic and no longer sticky. Shape into a ball. Put into greased bowl covered with greased plate and leave to rise in the warm for *20 minutes only*.

3. Re-knead on a floured surface then divide equally into 2 pieces. Roll each into a 16-inch (40-cm) oblong then roll up like a Swiss roll, starting from a long side. Point ends then place loaves across 2 large, lightly greased and floured baking trays. Make 5 or 6 diagonal slashes on top then brush with salted water.

4. Leave to rise in warm place for 1½ to 1¾ hours or until double in size. *Do not cover* as outsides need to dry out in order to be crisp when baked.

5. Bake 15 to 20 minutes just above oven centre set to 425°F (220°C), Gas 7. A dish of water in bottom of oven helps make the crusts extra crisp. Cool on a wire rack and eat fresh.

Rye Bread

Makes 1 loaf

1 level tblsp dried yeast with 1 level tsp caster sugar, honey or syrup OR 1 oz (25 g) fresh yeast and no sugar

6 fl. oz (175 ml) warm water (mix ²/₃ cold with ¹/₃ boiling)

4 oz (125 g) plain white strong flour

A speciality of Northern Europe and Scandinavia, this version with yogurt takes the place of the more characteristic use of what is termed 'sour dough' which is used as a starter.

1. Stir dried yeast and sugar, honey or syrup into the water. Leave in a warm place for 20 to 30 minutes or until frothy. Alternatively, blend fresh yeast with water.

2. Sift flour and salt into a bowl. Toss in rye flour then rub in lard or cooking fat.

3. Mix to a dough with yeast liquid and yogurt. Turn out on to a floured surface and knead 5 minutes.

1 level tsp salt
12 oz (350 g) rye flour
½ oz (15 g) lard or white
    cooking fat
1 carton (5 oz or 142 ml)
    natural yogurt

4. Put into a greased bowl, cover with a greased plate and leave to rise until double in size (for rising times, see points 7 and 8 of Basic Techniques.)

5. Re-knead on a floured surface then shape to fit a well greased 2-lb (900-g) oblong loaf tin.

6. Prick with a fork all over, cover with greased polythene or greaseproof paper and leave to rise in the warm for 35 to 40 minutes or until double in size.

7. Bake 45 minutes just above oven centre set to 400°F (200°C), Gas 6. Remove from tin and put on to a baking tray. Bake a further 7 minutes.

8. Transfer to a wire rack, cover with a tea towel and leave until cold.

Pitta Bread

Makes 8

2 level tsp dried yeast with
  1 level tsp caster sugar,
  honey or syrup OR ½ oz
  (15 g) fresh yeast and no
  sugar
½ pt (275 ml) warm water
  (mix ⅔ cold with ⅓
  boiling)
1 lb (450 g) plain white strong
  flour
1 level tsp salt

These are like flat loaves with pockets, eaten in the Middle East packed with kebabs (off their sticks), or served with taramosalata, hummus and tahina—a sesame seed and chickpea purée.

1. Stir dried yeast and sugar, honey or syrup into the water and leave in a warm place for 20 to 30 minutes or until frothy. Alternatively, blend fresh yeast with the water.

2. Sift flour and salt into a bowl. Mix to a dough with yeast liquid.

3. Turn out on to a floured surface and knead 10 to 15 minutes or until dough is smooth, elastic and no longer sticky.

4. Shape into a ball and put into an oiled bowl. Cover with an oiled plate and leave to rise until double in size. (For rising times, see points 7 and 8 of Basic Techniques.)

5. Re-knead dough until firm then divide equally into 8 pieces. Roll each into a 10 × 5-inch (25 × 12.5-cm) oblong.

6. Put on to 2 greased and floured baking trays. Cover with oiled polythene or greaseproof paper and leave to relax for 5 minutes only.

7. Bake 1 tray of Pittas at a time, placing it near top of very hot oven set to 475°F (240°C), Gas 9. Allow 6 to 8 minutes or until light brown.

8. Wrap Pittas in a damp tea towel to ensure soft crusts. Leave until cold then re-heat under hot grill for a few minutes before serving.

Chapati

Makes 8

8 oz (225 g) wholemeal flour
1 level tsp salt
6 fl. oz (175 ml) water

An unleavened Indian style bread used to scoop up curries.

1. Tip flour and salt into a bowl and mix to a soft dough with water.

2. Turn out on to a floured surface and knead a good 5 to 10 minutes or until dough is smooth and elastic. Shape into a ball, put into an oiled bowl and cover with an oiled plate. Leave 1 hour to relax.

3. Divide dough into 8 pieces and roll out very thinly on floured surface into 8-inch (20-cm) rounds. Gently shake off surplus flour.

4. Brush non-stick frying pan lightly with salad oil. When hot put in Chapatis, one at a time. Fry ½ minute. Turn over. Fry second side 1½ to 2 minutes or until lightly browned. Turn and cook first side for 1 more minute. (Press down the edges with a wooden spoon to encourage the dough to puff up.) Pile Chapatis, as they are cooked, in a clean tea towel. Serve warm, each folded in 4.

NON-YEASTED BREADS

Irish Soda Bread is a joy to eat freshly made and proves that *not* all good bread needs yeast! The other breads in this section depend on baking powder or self-raising flour for lightness and are fairly plain; cake-like in many respects, but not quite cakes.

Irish White Soda Bread

Makes 1 loaf or 4 'Farls'

8 oz (225 g) plain flour
1 level tsp bicarbonate of soda
½ level tsp salt
2 level tsp caster sugar
½ pt (275 ml) buttermilk
   (available from
   supermarket chains, foreign
   grocers and delicatessen
   shops)

Ireland's basic and most popular bread – eaten with virtually every meal from breakfast through to supper.

1. Sift flour, soda and salt into a bowl. Toss in sugar.

2. Mix to a soft dough with buttermilk.

3. Turn out on to a floured surface and knead quickly until smooth.

4. Shape into a 2-inch (5-cm) thick round and put on to a greased and floured baking tray.

5. Make a deepish crosscut on top then bake 20 to 25 minutes just above oven centre set to 425°F (220°C), Gas 7. The loaf is ready when it turns warm gold in colour.

6. Cool on a wire rack then split into 4 wedges or 'farls'. Slice and serve buttered. If possible, make and eat on the same day.

Makes 1 loaf or 4 'Farls'

Irish Brown Soda Bread

Closer in texture than White Soda Bread, this has a delicious flavour and is just as easy to make. All you do is substitute wholemeal for white flour and use 1¼ level teaspoons bicarbonate of soda.

Enriched Soda Breads

For a somewhat richer texture, rub 1 oz (25 g) butter, margarine, cooking fat or lard into the dry ingredients before adding buttermilk.

Spicy Banana Bread

Makes 1 loaf

6 oz (175 g) self-raising flour
½ level tsp salt
1 level tsp cinnamon
4 oz (125 g) caster sugar
1½ oz (40 g) walnuts, chopped
2 medium ripe bananas
1 Grade 3 egg, well beaten
1 oz (25 g) butter or margarine,
* melted*
2 to 4 tblsp milk

An ideal family cake-cum-bread, especially designed for tea-time or high-tea eating.

1. Grease and line a 1-lb (450 g) oblong loaf tin and line base and sides with greaseproof paper. Set oven to 350°F (180°C), Gas 4.

2. Sift flour, salt and cinnamon into a bowl. Toss in sugar and nuts.

3. Mash bananas finely. Mix thoroughly into dry ingredients with beaten egg and melted fat, and enough milk to form a semi-stiff mixture.

4. Spoon into prepared tin and bake 1 hour in oven centre. Turn out and cool on a wire rack. Slice when just cold and serve with butter or margarine.

Fruited Cider Bread

Makes 1 large loaf

12 oz (350 g) mixed dried fruit
¼ pt (150 ml) vintage cider
2 oz (50 g) preserved ginger,
  chopped
2 oz (50 g) glacé cherries,
  chopped
5 oz (150 g) light brown soft
  sugar
1 Grade 3 egg, beaten
8 oz (225 g) plain flour,
  sifted
2 level tsp baking powder,
  sifted

1. Put mixed dried fruit and cider into a bowl. Cover and leave to soak overnight. Stir in ginger and cherries.

2. Grease and line a 2-lb (900-g) oblong loaf tin. Set oven to 325°F (160°C), Gas 3.

3. Add sugar and egg to fruit mixture then gently fold into sifted flour and baking powder, already mixed in bowl.

4. When smoothly combined, transfer evenly to prepared tin.

5. Bake 1½ to 1¾ hours in oven centre. The bread is ready when a metal skewer, pushed gently into centre, comes out clean and dry.

6. Turn out and cool on a wire rack. Wrap in greaseproof paper then store in an airtight tin for 2 to 3 days before cutting.

Lincoln Plum Bread

Makes 1 large loaf

*4 oz (125 g) stoned prunes
hot strained tea
4 oz (125 g) butter or
    margarine (room
    temperature)
4 oz (125 g) demerara sugar
1 level tblsp black treacle
2 Grade 3 eggs (kitchen
    temperature)
1 tblsp brandy
7 oz (200 g) self-raising flour
½ level tsp salt
1 level tsp cinnamon
4 oz (125 g) EACH currants
    and sultanas*

1. Soak prunes in hot tea for 15 minutes. Drain and finely chop. While prunes are soaking, grease and paper-line a 2-lb (900-g) oblong loaf tin. Set oven to 275°F (140°C), Gas 1.

2. Cream butter or margarine with sugar and treacle until light and fluffy. Beat in eggs and brandy.

3. Sift together flour, salt and cinnamon then fold into the creamed ingredients alternately with currants and sultanas.

4. Gently stir in prunes. Spread smoothly into prepared tin and bake until golden brown in lower part of oven, allowing about 3½ to 4 hours. To test if bread is ready, push a metal skewer gently into the centre. If it comes out clean and dry, the loaf may be removed from the oven.

5. Leave in tin until cold before removing. Store in an airtight container about 2 to 3 days before cutting.

MISTAKES

Crust is thick and heavy
1. Bread baked too long at too low a temperature.

Top crust breaks away from loaf
1. Dough too wet.
2. Dough not covered while rising.
3. Dough not left to rise (or prove) for long enough.
4. Oven too hot.

Top crust flat instead of domed
1. Soft flour used.
2. Not enough salt added.
3. Too much liquid used.

Crust very pale
1. Oven not hot enough.
2. Sugar omitted.

Crust too dark
1. Oven too hot.
2. Too much sugar added.
3. Loaf baked too near top of oven.

Dough spills over tin
1. Tin too small.
2. Dough over-proved.

Loaf heavy
1. Soft flour used.
2. Too much salt added.
3. Dough under-kneaded.
4. Dough under-risen.
5. Dough left to rise in too warm a place.

Texture of loaf coarse, open and crumbly
1. Dough too wet.
2. Dough not kneaded enough.
3. Dough left to rise too much.
4. Oven not hot enough.

Dough has a strong yeast flavour
1. Fresh yeast stale.
2. Too much yeast used.
3. Dough allowed to rise for too long.

ACKNOWLEDGEMENTS

My warmest thanks to Len Burke and Jill Niblock of The Flour Advisory Bureau for their advice and help over many, many years. Without their assistance, this book would never have seen the light of day.

INDEX